weblinks

You don't need a computer to use this book. But, for readers who do have access to the Internet, the book provides links to recommended websites which offer additional information and resources on the subject.

You will find weblinks boxes like this on some pages of the book.

weblinks
For more music and dance careers advice, go to
www.waylinks.co.uk/
series/soyouwant/
musicanddance

waylinks.co.uk

To help you find the recommended websites easily and quickly, weblinks are provided on our own website, **waylinks.co.uk.** These take you straight to the relevant websites and save you typing in the Internet address yourself.

Internet safety

↗ Never give out personal details, which include: your name, address, school, telephone number, email address, password and mobile number.

↗ Do not respond to messages which make you feel uncomfortable – tell an adult.

↗ Do not arrange to meet in person someone you have met on the Internet.

↗ Never send your picture or anything else to an online friend without a parent's or teacher's permission.

↗ If you see anything that worries you, tell an adult.

A note to adults
Internet use by children should be supervised. We recommend that you install filtering software which blocks unsuitable material.

Website content

The weblinks for this book are checked and updated regularly. However, because of the nature of the Internet, the content of a website may change at any time, or a website may close down without notice. While the Publishers regret any inconvenience this may cause readers, they cannot be responsible for the content of any website other than their own.

HODDER
Wayland

So You Want to Work in

Music and Dance?

Margaret McAlpine

HODDER
Wayland

an imprint of Hodder Children's Books

First published in 2005 by Hodder Wayland,
an imprint of Hodder Children's Books

© Hodder Wayland 2005

Editor: Patience Coster
Inside design: Peta Morey
Cover design: Hodder Wayland

British Library Cataloguing Publication Data

McAlpine, Margaret
So you want to work in music and dance?
1. Music – Vocational guidance – Juvenile literature
2. Dance – Vocational guidance – Juvenile literature
I. Title
780.2'3

ISBN 0 7502 4582 4

Printed in China

Hodder Children's Books
A division of Hodder Headline Limited
338 Euston Road, London NW1 3BH

Picture Acknowledgements. The publishers would like to thank the following for
allowing their pictures to be reproduced in this publication:
Albert Ferreira/Reuters/Corbis 45; Ariel Skelley/Corbis 6, 28; Bob Daemmrich/
The Image Works/Topham 59 (*bottom*); Bob Krist/Corbis 24, 25; Bruce
Forster/Stone/Getty Images 43; Cathrine Wessel/Corbis 32; Cheryl Maeder/Corbis 14,
18; Christian Sarramon/Corbis 21; Chuck Savage/Corbis 13, 17, 22, 38;
Clive Barda/PAL/TopFoto 27 (*centre*); Colin McPherson/Corbis Sygma 36; Corbis 37;
Corbis Sygma 56; C. S. Langlois, Publiphoto Diffusion/Science Photo Library 52;
DiMaggio/Kalish/Corbis 55; Edward Holub/Corbis 44; Ethan Miller/Corbis 39, 51;
France Keyser/In Visu/Corbis 30; Françoise Gervais/Corbis 33; James L. Amos/Corbis 8;
James Marshall/Corbis 31; Jeff Zaruba/Corbis 29; Jim Craigmyle/Corbis 23;
Jon Feingersh/Corbis 40, 50; Kelly-Mooney Photography/Corbis 27 (*bottom*);
Larry Williams/Corbis 5; Layne Kennedy/Corbis 20; Macduff Everton/Corbis 46;
Mark E. Gibson/Corbis 16; Michael J. Doolittle/The Image Works/Topham 12;
Mitchell Gerber/Corbis 42, 48; Neal Preston/Corbis 41; Paul A. Souders/Corbis 10;
Penny Tweedie/Corbis 19; Richard Hutchings/Corbis 35 (*bottom*);
Robbie Jack/Corbis 4; Rowena Chowdrey/TopFoto 9; Sandra Rose/Getty Images 49;
Steve Sands/New York Newswire/Corbis 53; Stuart Hughes/Corbis 15;
Todd A. Gipstein/Corbis 57; Tom Stewart/Corbis 7, 35 (*centre*); TopFoto/UPPA 11, 47,
59 (*centre*); Topham Picturepoint 54.

Note: Photographs illustrating the 'day in the life of' pages are posed by models

Contents

Words in **bold** can be found in the glossary.

Dancer

What is a dancer?

Dancers tell a story or express emotions through the movement of their bodies. They usually dance to a musical accompaniment. Throughout the world and from the earliest times, human beings have used dance in religious ceremonies and to mark different events, such as weddings, funerals and battles. People have even used dance to try to change the weather.

Professional dancers perform three main types of dance:

Ballet dancers must follow a lengthy, highly disciplined and demanding training. This Russian dancer, Ekaterina Shipulina, is performing in the famous ballet, *Swan Lake.*

Classical or ballet
Classical dance can mean the traditional dances of countries around the world. In Europe and the USA, however, the term 'classical' has come to mean ballet dancing. Ballet was first performed in Italy in the early 1600s and the first ballet school was set up in France in 1681. While modern ballet is still based on the classical positions created in the seventeenth century, it uses these in new and exciting ways.

Musical theatre
This includes jazz, contemporary and modern dance and tap dancing. Tap developed in the USA and it combines Black American **step dancing** with the **clog dancing** of British and Irish immigrants.

Divine dancing

The Ancient Greeks believed that dancing was invented by the gods and it therefore became an important part of their religious worship. They believed that the gods had given the gift of dance to certain people, who in turn taught it to others. Early Greek dances often took place in a circle around a tree, an altar, or mystical objects. The people taking part believed that the dance freed them from evil.

Modern dance encourages freedom of expression, but still requires a disciplined approach. Modern dancers can find work in a range of musical productions in theatres, films and on cruise ships.

Contemporary

Early in the twentieth century, dancers such as Isadora Duncan turned away from ballet and developed their own forms of contemporary dance to express their emotions.

Main tasks of a dancer

It is not easy to earn a living as a professional dancer. The work is very competitive, which means a lot of people are chasing the same jobs. Most professional dancers begin dancing at a young age, taking lessons in a number of different dance forms such as ballet, jazz and tap. As they grow older, dancers specialize in a particular dance form.

A ballet teacher helps a young student find the correct position in a class for beginners.

● Dancers spend only a small amount of time performing. Most of their working life is taken up with hours of practice time spent on learning steps, rehearsing with other dancers, and exercising to keep their bodies at peak fitness.

Contemporary dance may look a great deal more relaxed than ballet, but it still involves long hours of practice and a high level of physical fitness.

Good points and bad points

'For me, dancing is a wonderful way of expressing my feelings and something that gives me a great deal of satisfaction.'

'To stay in peak physical condition, dancers need to be very strict with themselves. A career in dance would not suit a person who enjoys a hectic social life with late nights and junk food.'

- Most dancers work in the chorus or 'corps de ballet'. Dancers who are especially talented and dedicated to their work may become soloists and dance alone.

- In musical theatre, dancers are expected to be able to sing and act as well as dance.

- Choreographers create dance routines by designing a script or **score** for dancers. Their job is to make the movements as interesting as possible, while ensuring that the dance fits the music. Choreographers have often trained as dancers themselves.

- Choreographers work with dancers in rehearsals, developing dances for public performances. Some choreographers plot every step the dancers are to take, while others allow the dancers to experiment and work out their own movements.

Dance is a very competitive career and few dancers reach the top. However, as a hobby, dance is a great way for people to exercise and express themselves.

weblinks

For more information about a career as a dancer, go to www.waylinks.co.uk/series/soyouwant/musicanddance

Skills needed to be a dancer

Talent

Dancers need to have strong, natural dance skills. They must carry themselves gracefully and have a good sense of timing, rhythm, imagination and creativity, which they can express through the movement of their bodies. In musical productions which use modern dancers, such as *West Side Story*, *Moulin Rouge* and *Cats*, acting and singing skills are equally as important as dancing skills.

Dancers need a good sense of timing and rhythm, but they also need a huge amount of stamina and physical strength.

Commitment and determination

The life of a dancer is tough. It involves hours of practice often in cold, draughty rehearsal rooms. Dancing is an insecure profession and dancers often have to manage on very little money. They have to be able to cope with disappointment and criticism and still carry on. Many young people struggle to make a career for themselves as dancers. Talent does not guarantee success, and many gifted dancers fail to make a living and have to find other jobs.

Here tap dancers perform in a musical production for the theatre. As with other forms of dance, tap dancers need to perfect a range of complicated steps but should make their performance seem effortless.

Physical strength and stamina
Dancing is as energetic and physically demanding as sports such as athletics. A dancer needs to have a strong back and strong legs. Dancers need to take regular exercise to keep physically fit. Diet is important because weight gain can result in lack of work.

Appearance
Most professional dancers have a particular appearance, with long legs and slim bodies. They also need to be the right height, not too tall and not too small.

fact file

Some dancers start dancing as children and begin serious training by the age of sixteen years or even younger. Specialist dance schools take children as young as eleven years of age and combine dancing with a general education. Other dancers attend ordinary schools and take dance lessons in their own time. On leaving school, they go on to take a full-time dance performance course at a specialist dance college. To gain a place, students need to pass an interview, an **audition** and a medical examination.

A day in the life of a dancer

Sean Myers

Sean is hoping to make a career as a modern dancer. He began dancing when he was eleven years old, and is currently employed part-time in a sandwich bar to earn additional money.

6.00 am   I set off for my job working in a sandwich bar. It's not the greatest job in the world, but it fits in with the rest of my life and means that I earn some regular money.

10.00 am   My dance class begins. Although I've finished my full-time training, I still take classes to improve the standard of my dancing. There's always something new to learn.

12.30 pm   I have a coffee and a sandwich with friends from the class. It's a good opportunity to exchange gossip and news about possible work.

2.00 pm   I start making phone calls, getting details of auditions that might lead to work. I'm waiting to hear the results of an audition I went for a few days ago. The job involves working as a dancer for six months on a cruise liner.

There is a lot of competition for dance work. Here, young ballet dancers wait for their turn to audition for a production of The Nutcracker in Seattle, USA.

The definition of dance has broadened in recent times to include many different elements. Here, a modern performance incorporates various new acrobatic dance forms, such as breakdancing, pop, 'lock', swing, tap and boogaloo.

There are good opportunities in the leisure industry because holiday-makers want to be entertained. Large cruise liners have their own theatres on board and put on shows every night. From my point of view, work on a ship would be great. My meals and a bed would be provided and I'd have the opportunity to work as a professional dancer.

2.30 pm I visit the dance studio and do some exercises to make sure my legs and arms remain flexible and supple.

4.30 pm I pluck up my courage and ring the agent who is running the auditions for the cruise liner job. She wants me to call round in a couple of days. I've got to be realistic and not hope for too much, but I can't help feeling excited.

Disc Jockey

What is a disc jockey?

A disc jockey, or DJ, entertains audiences by playing recorded music and by commenting on the latest events in the music scene. DJs often make their own original **mixes** of two or more tracks of music and break these up with conversation and jokes.

The work of a DJ falls into three main groups:

Mobile DJs
Most DJs fit into this group. They work at parties and private celebrations, providing the entertainment throughout the event and selecting the music to suit the audience. Mobile DJs are responsible for setting up and clearing away their equipment, which will include a **mixing desk**, vinyl (records) and CDs, **amplifiers**, speakers and lighting.

A young DJ at work at Yale University's radio station. DJs often polish their craft by working initially for radio stations based in colleges or hospitals.

Radio DJs
These DJs usually work on radio stations which produce largely music-based programmes. Radio DJs have to keep to a very tight timescale, chatting to the listeners in between tracks and sometimes reading news, commercials and travel and weather bulletins. Their job also includes phone-in sessions (talking to listeners over the air) and conducting interviews with well-known personalities.

The rise of the disc jockey

The first time a record was played over the airwaves was in 1906. The first commercial radio stations started in 1920 in Pittsburgh, USA. Before the arrival of television, radio was popular and radio personalities were paid very high salaries for that time.

In the 1940s and 1950s, most of the programmes on many radio stations were fronted by disc jockeys who would play their choice of music. It was not until the 1980s that individual disc jockeys became famous in their own right, and began to influence the sales of records by recommending them and playing them on their shows.

Club DJs

These DJs are based in nightclubs where people come to dance and to listen to a particular type of music. Their job is to keep the audience entertained and dancing. Club DJs put together their own performances using different pieces of music. Popular DJs are a big draw and people come to clubs especially to hear them.

Many DJs have their own equipment and drive from place to place, providing the music for private parties and other functions.

Main tasks of a disc jockey

Very few DJs become famous, and even those who do become successful tend not to stay in the work for very long. They often move on into other areas of entertainment, or they take jobs with record companies. Around 50 per cent of DJs work part-time and have another job from which they earn regular money.

This DJ is 'scratching' a disc to produce a particular sound and rhythm.

DJs do not simply play music tracks. Most of them, especially the mobile and club DJs, use a range of different techniques to achieve the effects they want.

- DJs use mixing techniques – this involves combining two or more music tracks together and moving quickly from one turntable to another.

- They also use scratching techniques – moving the record turntables by hand in order to vary their speed. This is a complicated process involving more than 60 different techniques.

Good points and bad points

'I love being able to play my kind of music and seeing people up and dancing and having a great time.'

'This may be hard to believe, but the worst thing about my job is the loneliness. I work as a club DJ from about 8.00 pm to 4.00 am and then I go home to sleep. When I'm at work I'm too busy playing music to talk to people.'

- They use cueing – starting music at a particular place on the disc.

- DJs need to keep up with all the technical developments, including those in lighting and multimedia. These developments, such as the introduction of strobe lighting and digital music, happen very quickly. Lighting and musical equipment in clubs is often highly technical and sophisticated.

- DJs spend a lot of time listening to new music in order to keep up-to-date. Famous DJs receive dozens of sample tapes and new albums every week from musicians, their agents and promoters in the hope that they will be played on the radio and in clubs.

- Wherever they work, DJs need to build up their audience and play the type of music their listeners want to hear. This is not as easy as it sounds and behind the relaxed attitude of many DJs is a great deal of organization and attention to detail.

This nightclub DJ is using a computer to produce music digitally. In this way, DJs can modify and transfer music tracks from vinyl to CD.

Skills needed to be a disc jockey

A passion for music
DJs spend a great deal of their time either playing or listening to music. They need to enjoy doing this and be interested in the music they play.

Technical skills
DJs must deal confidently with complicated sound and lighting equipment. Mobile DJs need to know how to set up their equipment and dismantle it and pack it away when they have finished. If a problem arises with the equipment, it is up to the DJ to put it right as quickly as possible.

Creativity
Mobile and club DJs especially need to be able to make their own music from music. Experienced DJs use turntables as musical instruments and combine several tracks together to make a new sound. It takes a lot of practice to do this successfully.

Radio DJs may need to follow a script or notes for their programmes. The script will have been prepared in advance, usually by them or in conjunction with their producer.

Organizational skills
All DJs, but especially those working on the radio, have to plan their programmes down to the last second because the time schedule is very tight and programmes must not run over their time or finish too early.

A good DJ can be the making of a great party.

Entertainment skills

DJs need to capture the attention of their audience and make sure people are enjoying themselves. This involves chatting about records, telling jokes and making the audience feel relaxed.

Determination

A DJ's life is tough, and few of them become famous. Many less determined DJs may give up the work for jobs that offer more security.

fact file

There are no set routes to becoming a DJ. Some people begin by working voluntarily with community radio stations. Once they have developed their own style they send off CDs of their performance to club managers, promoters and agents. Mobile DJs need to save enough money to buy their own equipment.

Adaptability

Working as a DJ can be a lonely existence, especially for those on the night shift. It means being awake when most people are asleep and sleeping when the rest of the world is at work.

A day in the life of a disc jockey

Jack Gilmore

Jack works as a DJ on a local radio station. He started his career as a mobile DJ, playing at parties and local events. His reputation grew, and after two years he was offered a nightly radio slot.

2.00 pm I work the night slot, so my day begins in the afternoon. I get up, have some breakfast and listen to the radio. I try to listen as much as I can because I learn a lot from other DJs.

6.00 pm I go into the radio station for a chat with the producer. Although the station is small, we keep ourselves busy and get involved with a lot of community events. The producer and I talk over the dates of some appearances I'm booked to make. They include judging at a school music festival, opening a charity fete and doing some disc-jockeying at a youth festival. We discuss ways to promote these events on my programme.

7.30 pm I start to plan my programme. I need to have a good idea of the shape it will take, although nothing works out exactly as planned.

DJs must be completely familiar with the technology they operate to ensure that their presentations run without a hitch.

DJs need to be well-organized and must plan their programmes carefully. Timings and schedules are worked out down to the last second.

10.00 pm   I'm waiting to go on air. On the night slot it's usually easy listening that people want, but I try to include the odd surprise item, such as some unusual listener requests. A lot of people listen to night-time radio: shift workers, car drivers, and parents with young babies who keep them awake.

12.00 am   At midnight we start the phone-in slot, when I ask listeners to ring in with requests or to give their opinion of something in the news. This keeps me on my toes, because I never know what people will say next. I keep my eye on the clock because I have to give news reports every hour, on the hour.

4.30 am   My replacement arrives and I sign off.

Instrument Maker/Repairer

What is an instrument maker/repairer?

Instrument makers/ repairers design, make, restore and mend musical instruments.

Instrument makers range from individual craftsmen who are self-employed and working alone to huge international manufacturing companies. Individual instrument makers are responsible for making the entire instrument and assembling the different parts. Instrument makers working in mass production usually undertake one part of the work on a particular section of the production line, using specialized machinery.

Professional musicians need to play on the highest quality instruments they can afford. They usually play handcrafted instruments made by skilled craftspeople and costing a great deal of money. At present there is a growing interest in period or historical instruments which are individually made. Most people who play musical instruments, however, do so for pleasure and are happy to play mass-produced instruments that cost far less than those that are individually made.

Choosing the right material is important because this can affect the tone of the instrument. This violin maker in his workshop in Wisconsin, USA, creates instruments from wood brought up from the bottom of Lake Superior. This wood is very **pliable** because it has been soaked in water for so long.

The beginnings of music

The first musical sounds were probably made by early humans hitting objects. It is likely that they discovered by accident how to make different sounds, for example, by blowing a pipe, a reed, a piece of bamboo or animal bones. As time went on, people began to notice different **pitches** and to make instruments that could produce different notes.

Instrument repairers include piano tuners, who adjust the tension of the piano strings to the correct pitch. They need a good ear in order to know if an instrument is properly tuned.

Instrument repairers respond to calls for assistance from people who own instruments that need attention. They check instruments regularly and repair them when necessary.

Instrument makers may also repair musical instruments. They usually specialize in a particular type of instrument such as: brass (including trumpets, horns and trombones); woodwind (including flutes, clarinets, oboes, saxophones and recorders); strings (including violins, violas, cellos and double bass); keyboards (pianos, organs); and electric guitars.

Main tasks of an instrument maker/repairer

Making and repairing musical instruments is highly skilled work that calls for accuracy and great attention to detail. Instruments are often made for a particular musician who will discuss with the instrument maker exactly what he or she wants.

The instrument maker must then:

- make drawings of the instruments;
- select the correct materials, such as the right type of wood;
- prepare them, for example, by cutting and soaking wood to make it pliable, by shaping wooden parts for stringed instruments, or by making parts such as mouthpieces for brass instruments;
- assemble the parts, for example, by glueing or screwing wooden parts and **welding** or **soldering** brass sections;
- fix electrical parts to electrical instruments.

When it comes to buying a musical instrument, a lot of thought goes into selecting the right one. An instrument with poor tone can discourage the player from practising.

Good points and bad points

'I am quite musical, so working with instruments is always a pleasure. I like discussing with musicians what exactly they want and then making the right instrument for them. It gives me a lot of satisfaction.'

'As a freelance instrument repairer, my work is insecure. Sometimes I take on too much work and at other times I don't have enough.'

The instrument repairer's job depends on the type of instrument that needs to be repaired.

- The repairer will service woodwind instruments every one to two years. He or she will remove the dust and fluff behind the keys, replace worn pads and oil rod screws.
- The repairer will eventually re-laquer or re-plate brass instruments and service the valves. He or she will also mend leaks or blockages in the tubing.
- The repairer of stringed instruments deals with two types: fretted instruments, such as guitars and mandolins; and unfretted instruments, such as violins and cellos. (Frets are the wooden or metal ridges on the fingerboard of a stringed instrument on to which the strings are pressed to make different notes.) Repairs include mending cracks in the wooden bodywork, fitting new **bridges** and refitting **pegs**.

Professional musicians spend a great deal of money on buying instruments made by specialist craftspeople.

- The repairer of keyboard instruments, such as pianos and harpsichords, needs to tune them regularly to make sure the notes are true. He or she does this by adjusting the strings inside the body of the instrument to the correct pitch, using a tuning fork and special hammer, known as a turning lever. Damaged black and white keys may also need replacing.

Skills needed to be an instrument maker/repairer

An interest in music

Musical instrument makers and repairers need to be able to discuss with customers exactly what they want. It would be difficult for them to do this without any knowledge of music. If they can appreciate the job their instruments will do, it also makes their work more satisfying.

A good ear

Good hearing and a highly trained ear are necessary so instrument makers can tune musical instruments and make sure that the pitch and tone are accurate.

A high level of practical skills

Instrument makers work with wood and metal and need to know how to use these materials in a skilful manner.

Knowledge of electronics

Today many instruments are electric, which means the instrument is plugged into a machine called an amplifier to make it sound louder. Instrument makers specializing in electronic instruments, such as electric guitars, need to have good knowledge of electronics.

This piano maker is adjusting the tones of a grand piano at the Steinway & Sons factory in New York City.

Patience

Nobody makes a musical instrument quickly. The work is slow and every step needs to be checked and re-checked. To produce a high quality instrument,

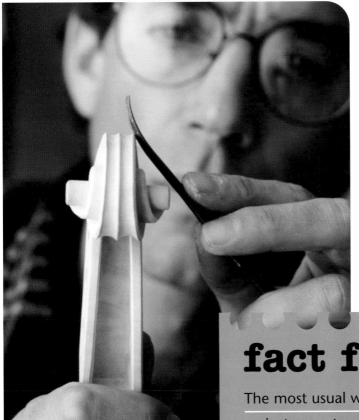

This violin maker is using a small tool called a file to sand the scroll at the end of the neck of a violin.

fact file

The most usual way to become an instrument maker/repairer is to take a degree or diploma course at a university or college.

there can be no mistakes. An instrument that is nearly but not quite right is not good enough.

Good business skills

Many musical instrument makers/repairers are self-employed. This means they have to run the financial side of their work, keeping accounts and working out exactly how much to charge for a job.

weblinks

For more information on a career as an instrument maker/repairer, go to www.waylinks.co.uk/series/soyouwant/musicanddance

A day in the life of an instrument maker/repairer

Will Jackson

Will makes and repairs stringed musical instruments. He originally trained as a carpenter and joiner and made furniture. He made his first guitar using an instruction book. Gradually his reputation as an instrument maker grew and he began getting requests to make guitars for other people.

8.30 am   I picked up a consignment of wood, strings and pegs early this morning and I am just unloading the materials from my van.

9.00 am   This is what I enjoy doing most, working away in my workshop. There is something almost magical about turning a piece of wood into an instrument capable of producing great music. At the moment I'm putting the finishing touches to a violin which has been ordered by a German musician. I take orders from all over the world.

10.00 am   I receive a phone call from a woman who teaches the harp. She wants to know if I can make some small harps for her pupils. I suggest we get together with some sketches and talk over the project. After fifteen years of instrument making, I'm now confident enough to design many types of musical instrument myself.

1.00 pm   After a morning in the workshop, I'm ready for a break and lunch.

2.30 pm I check over some notes for a new job I'm about to start. Taking into account the musician's requirements, I calculate the materials I'm going to need. Materials need to be ordered from a specialist supplier and delivery can take some time, so I email over my requests straight away.

6.30 pm Time to lock up and find out what the rest of the world has been doing.

There is great satisfaction in hearing an instrument you have created making music.

This instrument maker is constructing a guitar at a workshop in New Jersey, USA.

Music Teacher

Music teachers train other people to read music and play instruments or learn to sing. Most music teachers are skilled musicians who have a thorough knowledge of **musical theory** and techniques. They can usually play at least one musical instrument or, in the case of singing teachers, can sing to a high standard. Many musicians find they gain almost as much satisfaction from teaching music to others as from performing themselves.

In schools, music is taught as a class subject. In primary schools, music teachers may teach other general subjects as well as music, while still being responsible for school musical productions and concerts. Teachers in upper and high schools teach music at different levels to suit the interests and

Music teachers make music fun for young children.

Amazing Mozart

One of the world's greatest musicians, Wolfgang Amadeus Mozart, was born in Austria in 1756. At the age of five he was already composing music and he wrote his first symphony at the age of nine. While still a child, Mozart was taken on a musical tour of Europe and played at many European royal courts. He went on to compose many operas and symphonies, but died in poverty in 1791 at the age of thirty-five.

abilities of their pupils. They prepare pupils to take school curriculum and individual voice or instrumental examinations. They also coach school orchestras, choirs and music groups.

Peripatetic music teachers visit different schools giving instrumental or singing lessons to pupils with particular talent, preparing them for music examinations. These lessons are paid for either by the education authority or the pupils' parents.

Some music teachers give private music lessons in their own homes or those of their pupils. Professional musicians may also teach classes to earn extra money.

Learning a musical instrument can help to build children's confidence.

Main tasks of a music teacher

Music teachers working in schools encourage all pupils, not only those with strong musical ability, to enjoy and appreciate music at their own level. Their work includes:

● teaching pupils the theory of music and explaining the principles behind music-making, including how to read music and how to write it down;

Music teachers in schools and colleges are usually responsible for musical productions and concerts.

Good points and bad points

'I enjoy my work and it is a pleasure to see young people make progress with their music.'

'As a music teacher my days are quite complicated. I teach part-time in two different schools and also give some lessons in my own home. This means keeping a close watch on the time and checking my diary carefully every day.'

- introducing pupils to different types of music such as classical, jazz and folk music and helping them to understand how music has developed over the years;

- teaching groups to sing songs together and to make music using percussion instruments that are simple to play and make a sound when they are shaken or hit with a hand or a stick (percussion instruments include drums, bells, cymbals and maracas);

- organizing school music productions. Most schools with pupils between the ages of five and eighteen years put on musical events and concerts during the school year. Often these events bring together different departments in productions that include music, dance and drama. On these occasions, music, art and drama teachers may work closely together as a group.

Talented pupils may receive extra tuition. Teachers may provide musical accompaniment for vocalists or instrumental soloists during their examinations.

As well as teaching music as a general subject in schools, music teachers give lessons individually to pupils who have particular musical ability or interests. These lessons are generally at a higher level than the class sessions and involve:

- preparing pupils for examinations in music and for auditions for entry to music schools or colleges;

- training school choirs, orchestras, music groups and soloists to take part in music productions, competitions and festivals.

Skills needed to be a music teacher

Love of music
Music teachers need to be inspired by a real love of music if they are to make the subject interesting and enjoyable to other people.

A high level of musical skill and knowledge
Teachers need to have studied music at a high level. They should be able to play competently so that they can demonstrate practical musical skills and technique to their students.

Strong communication skills
Music teachers need to share their love of music with their students. All pupils, whatever their ability, should find music fun and enjoy their lessons. Teachers should therefore be able to convey the subject in a lively way. They also teach musical theory to pupils studying at an advanced level, so need to explain complicated information clearly in a way that can be understood.

At music college or university, students are taught at an advanced level. They develop a detailed knowledge of music theory and are usually required to compose original pieces of music.

Enthusiasm
All teachers need to be enthusiastic in order for their classes to be lively and interesting. Music teachers should create an atmosphere of creativity where everyone feels confident enough to take part in the activities.

Flexibility
Not all pupils are the same, and music teachers need to approach the subject in different ways.

weblinks
For more information on a career as a music teacher, go to
www.waylinks.co.uk/series/soyouwant/musicanddance

Some classes enjoy music for fun while others study the theory and history of music at an advanced level. Teachers need to adapt their teaching methods to suit each class or individual pupil.

Discipline skills
Teachers need to control groups of children and young people in a firm but fair way.

fact file

Music teachers working in state schools must be trained and qualified as teachers as well as having musical qualifications, such as a degree in music. This means studying music at an advanced level at a university or music college.

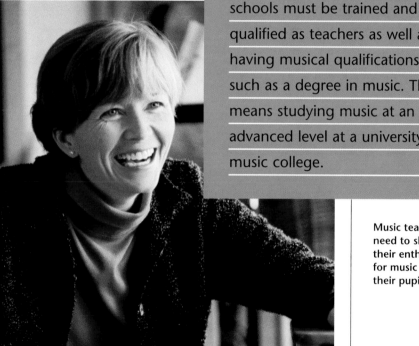

Music teachers need to share their enthusiasm for music with their pupils.

Kate Frost

Kate teaches music in local schools and in her own home. She has a degree in music and is also a trained teacher.

9.00 am   I begin my day in the classroom with a group of seven-year-old students. We're making musical instruments today and have a great selection of tins, plastic bottles and metal plates.

9.30 am   It's noisy but fun playing our instruments. The children want to use them again so I make a note of this in my lesson planner.

10.30 am   My class of seven-year-olds needs to practise some French songs for a concert in three weeks' time. They've learned the words with the French teacher and now we try adding the music.

11.30 am   The head teacher wants to see me about working some extra hours.

12.00 pm   I'm teaching at home this afternoon, so I hurry back to prepare for my first pupil.

1.30 pm   My student Liz has two children and when they started school she decided to learn the piano. She is making great progress and it's fun teaching her.

2.45 pm   I take ten minutes' break before my next pupils arrive. They are two four-year-olds whose parents want them to enjoy music from a young age. Both their mothers stay with them and we all sing nursery rhymes, bang on drums and have a noisy time.

4.30 pm   James arrives for his lesson. He is fifteen years old and is having extra help after an illness. We catch up with some theory and then James plays the piano and we discuss his technique. He needs a lot of encouragement to build up his confidence.

6.00 pm   I make notes on my pupils' progress before finishing for the day.

The advanced level of music teaching involves musical **notation** (writing down what is heard).

You are never too young to enjoy making music.

Musician

What is a musician?

Musicians play a musical instrument or sing. Professional musicians make a living doing this, while semi-professional musicians earn some money in this way, but do other jobs as well.

Music is divided into two main types: classical and popular. However this does not mean all music falls clearly into one of these groups. For example, some scores for film sound-tracks are considered by many people to be modern classics.

- Classical music is written down using musical notation. Classical musicians follow the composer's written instructions carefully, which means they perform in the way the composer intended. There is little opportunity for performers to **improvise** or create their own music from the original piece.

Classical musicians read the music they play. These orchestral musicians are discussing a passage from the German composer Wagner's *Ring Cycle.*

Classical musicians follow a formal academic training to a high level. Unlike popular music, classical music does not usually form a background to other activities, such as dancing. Audiences generally listen to classical music in silence.

- Popular (pop) music is usually very popular with music fans for a brief period of time. It is sometimes written using musical notation, but is often recorded

The King

Rock legend Elvis Presley died in 1977, but he remains one of the world's best-selling music artists today. Over one billion of his records have been sold, the highest number ever sold by any artist. Every year, more than 600,000 fans visit his Graceland home near Memphis, Tennessee, to honour the man who has become known as 'The King'.

as it is being composed and developed by adding and removing sections from the recording. Pop music covers a wide range of different types of music, including folk, blues, country and western, **reggae** and **hip-hop**. With certain types of pop music, such as jazz, the musicians often improvise and make additions to the original piece. Pop music often involves electronic sound techniques and **amplification**. The music is promoted to achieve commercial success by being sold on CDs and played on radio and television. Pop music is also played live at concerts, festivals and in clubs.

While many pop musicians will have taken music lessons and/or some kind of training, others may not have had a formal music training but will have taught themselves or learned in an informal way.

Elvis Presley, shown here in the early part of his career, has been one of the most successful artists in the history of the pop music industry.

Main tasks of a musician

Whether musicians are of a classical or popular discipline, they need to spend long hours practising and attending rehearsals. Work is uncertain for all but a handful of top musicians, and most are self-employed. A few, but not many, classical musicians have permanent **contracts** with orchestras.

Classical musicians aim to earn a living by:

- giving live musical performances in front of an audience;
- making recordings in studios.

It is difficult to find such work all of the time, so many classical musicians also:

- work on backing tracks for advertisements and films;
- teach part-time either with individual private pupils or in schools.

Classical orchestras tend to perform music that has been written by a composer. Each instrument will have been given its own part to follow.

Good points and bad points

'I've been a professional classical singer for five years. I've performed at some important events. I love performing and feel my career is moving forward.'

'I still don't earn enough to support myself and have to rely on doing casual jobs in restaurants. Most of my singing work is freelance and, like most performers, I don't have any job security.'

A very small number of musicians become soloists, but the majority perform as part of an orchestra, **chamber group**, ensemble or choir. Some classical musicians are also composers, writing their own musical works; others become **conductors**.

All classical musicians need to practise for several hours each day. They also need to maintain their instruments in perfect condition and keep up-to-date with music theory.

Popular musicians aim to earn a living by:

- performing a particular type of music such as pop, jazz, folk or 'easy listening';
- recording music in studios for albums, videos and CDs;
- giving live performances at concerts, clubs and outdoor venues.

Popular musicians either work solo, or as part of a duo (two musicians), or as part of a group or band. Some popular musicians sing and dance as part of their act and many compose their own work. Except for a small minority, many popular musicians supplement their income with money from other work, such as jobs in bars, restaurants and shops.

Pop musicians often achieve success by reflecting current youth trends. Here the Backstreet Boys perform a rap routine in Las Vegas, USA.

Skills needed to be a musician

Classical and popular musicians need:

A great deal of musical talent
No matter what sort of music a musician plays, standards are high. A great many gifted musicians want to become professional and only a few of the most talented succeed.

Determination
A tiny proportion of musicians may have a lucky break early in their careers, but in general earning a living as a professional musician is very tough. There are a lot of disappointments to be faced. Musicians must be prepared to hear their work criticized and not let this dent their enthusiasm and determination to carry on.

Jazz musicians tend to enjoy working as part of a group because it gives them the opportunity to improvise with other musicians.

Dedication
Even the most talented musicians need to put in hours of practice every day. This, combined with the need for part-time work in order to earn money, means that few musicians have time to relax and enjoy a social life.

Teamwork
All musicians, including soloists, work as part of a team, whether they are in a pop group, an orchestra or a choir. This means they must be aware of other people's needs, be cheerful and reliable and prepared to do as they are told. There is no place in the music world for difficult people who do not work well in a group. The media might run

Only the most gifted musicians become soloists. This is the world famous jazz trumpeter Wynton Marsalis performing in Santiago, Chile.

stories about pop stars who throw tantrums, but even the rich and famous risk losing work if they are bad-tempered and unreliable.

Business skills
As freelancers, most musicians are responsible for dealing with their own business affairs. This means they need to keep track of bookings and produce well-maintained accounts of the money they earn and spend.

fact file

Classical musicians need to take a lengthy musical education, usually including postgraduate study at a music college or university. There is no set training for popular musicians, although diploma and degree courses in popular music are available. Musicians need to gain as much experience as possible performing live and sending demo tapes to music companies.

A day in the life of a professional musician

Jenny Chow

Jenny plays the violin. She studied music at university, then took a course in performance music, to learn how to play in public. She has been working professionally for five years.

9.00 am I'm packing my case and feeling really excited because I start a music tour tomorrow, which means nearly three months' work. I'm joining a group of musicians and we will be giving concerts in the grounds of castles, country houses and colleges throughout the summer. It's a full schedule and we'll be doing a lot of travelling, so I need to be well organized.

9.30 am Time to practise. I have a list of the music we are going to perform during the season. I've been practising the pieces for hours to make sure my playing is up to standard. The first few days the musicians get together will be spent in rehearsal, but I must make sure I'm confident with the music before I start playing as part of a group.

Professional musicians travel to wherever there is work. Here country singer Willie Nelson steps down from his tour bus.

---

weblinks

For more information
on a career as a musician,
go to
www.waylinks.co.uk/series/
soyouwant/musicanddance

Outdoor concerts are popular during the summer months. Here the Oregon Symphony Orchestra performs in a waterfront park.

12.30 pm I take a break from practising to do some packing and to email my itinerary to my parents. They have always supported me and plan to come to a couple of concerts over the summer.

2.30 pm I receive a phone call from the organizer to check that I'll be arriving with my violin and luggage tomorrow.

3.00 pm I need to practise for a further couple of hours, then I should be just about ready for the rehearsals with the other musicians.

5.30 pm I put my violin away, finish my packing and get ready to meet some friends for a meal and a chance to say goodbye until the autumn.

Promotions Manager

What is a promotions manager?

The job of a promotions manager in the music industry is to gain as much publicity as possible for a particular musician or a group. The promotions manager's work includes sorting out contracts and organizing music tours and personal appearances. Some promotions managers are self-employed while others work for particular venues, such as nightclubs, making sure the popular artists they feature will attract large audiences, and setting up publicity for these events.

The popular music industry is overcrowded with artists wanting to get to the top. Talent is often not enough and that is where the promotions manager comes in, giving musicians the best breaks possible. No matter how good a recording is, people need to hear it before they decide to go out and buy it. It is difficult for new groups and musicians to get their names known and recognized. Once an artist or group has achieved some degree of success, they might have help promoting themselves from a promotions manager.

Promotions managers working for nightclubs need to bring in a large number of people to cover costs.

Promotions teams

International pop stars such as Madonna employ a large number of staff to run their promotions industry. The work of the promotions team includes organizing world tours and supervising the production of support material, which ranges from calendars, books and photographs to clothes and toys.

Pop stars like Madonna, shown here on world tour in 2004, depend on a large team of people to book venues, advertise the coming event, deal with the press and promote the artist's work.

Wherever they work, promotions managers aim to attract as much attention as they can. To do this they need to build up excellent contacts with the media. They have to be on good terms with a great many people and need to put a lot of energy into their work.

Main tasks of a promotions manager

Promotions managers take care of administrative work. This includes:

- discussing contracts and getting the best possible deal for the musicians they represent;
- organizing promotional material, such as leaflets and flyers, and arranging for them to be sent out to nightclubs, music shops, and handed out to interested passers-by in the street;
- keeping paperwork up-to-date and making sure that artists are where they should be;
- checking any legal concerns that arise from matters such as cancelled performances or sickness;
- making sure activities are kept within an agreed budget.

Billboard advertising, like this promoting a concert by a world-leading operatic tenor at the historic site of Angkor in Cambodia, plays an important part in attracting audiences to music events.

Good points and bad points

'I'm an energetic person who enjoys being busy, which is why my jobs suits me. I don't mind working long hours and I get along with most people.'

'I do need a thick skin sometimes, because if anything goes wrong, for example, problems at a gig, I'm the one who takes the blame.'

Promotions managers working for an artist or a group have to try as many ways as possible to get them noticed by the media. This involves:

- persuading newspapers and magazines to interview artists and persuading television and radio stations to interview them and play their recordings;
- arranging appearances at record signings, nightclubs and charity events;
- checking on the best moment to release a record, avoiding times when the charts will be full of other famous names;
- organizing tours.

Promotions managers working for a venue, such as a nightclub, need to bring in as many people as possible through its doors. They must:

- know their audience and book acts that will be popular;
- organize promotional activities and material such as leaflets, flyers, t-shirts and balloons to give away in order to advertise events;
- make sure events run smoothly and the venue is safe with all safety exits free;
- check that legal requirements are met (for example, clubs are only allowed to admit a certain number of people at a time).

Promotions managers try to ensure that their clients appear in the best possible light. This may involve booking them for charity events. Here members of the US pop group BB MAK pose for the camera at a celebrity auction in support of Crusaid, a charity supporting people with HIV and AIDS.

Skills needed to be a promotions manager

A strong interest in the music industry
Promotions managers need a good knowledge and understanding of the music industry to book successful concert tours for musicians and to organize the right type of events for nightclubs.

An outgoing personality
It is not easy making contacts in tough and competitive fields like the music industry and the media. Promotions managers must be confident, lively and able to work with all sorts of people, from musicians and technicians to journalists and fans.

Patience
Some pop stars are not easy to deal with, especially when things go wrong. Promotions managers need to be able to stay calm and take criticism, even when they feel they don't deserve it.

An eye for detail
It is up to the promotions manager to ensure everything runs smoothly. This means checking hotel bookings and tour venues, and making sure that transport is available by, for example, booking plane and train tickets. Those working for a nightclub need to check bookings, costings and publicity.

In the late 1970s, Malcolm McLaren (centre) made a name for himself as a record producer and promotions manager who played a leading role in popularizing punk rock.

Television coverage is great publicity. Here, the rap artist Ludacris is interviewed as he arrives for a festival in aid of a charity supporting disadvantaged children.

Communication and negotiating skills

Promotions managers need to be very **tenacious** and persuasive. They must convince DJs and television presenters to play certain records or interview a particular musician on their shows.

Financial skills

By agreeing fees for shows and appearances, promotions managers need to get the best possible deal for their clients.

fact file

There is no set route for becoming a promotions manager, though some have music qualifications, business diplomas or degrees. The way in usually involves taking a very junior job, for example, doing office work or running errands in the music industry. This way, the person can learn as much as possible before applying for more responsible jobs.

Lynn Brady

Lynn works as a promotions manager for a nightclub. She worked for a public relations agency after leaving university and before taking her present job.

9.30 am I check through some leaflets I've had designed to publicize coming events at the club. I notice two of the dates are wrong and phone the printer. I ask to see a corrected leaflet before I agree to printing. The printer doesn't like it. He wants to put the mistakes right and print straight away, but I can't afford to take any risks.

10.15 am I receive a phone call from a television producer. He's making a film about entertainment in the area and wants to shoot some footage in the club. It sounds like great publicity to me and I arrange for us to meet for lunch tomorrow.

11.00 am I'm planning activities six months ahead. I know the names I'd like to book and start ringing agents and managers to get some idea of when their clients are free and what their charges would be.

Successful publicity can fill a nightclub.

Promotions managers target fans by organizing news stories, photographs and appearances. Here Justin Timberlake and J C Chasez shake hands with fans as they arrive for the Billboard Music Awards.

12.45 pm I have lunch with the music editor of a newspaper. We've been friends for quite a while and I'm hoping he will give me some coverage for the club's coming programme.

2.00 pm We have a visit from a member of the fire brigade to check that our fire exits and alarm systems are in order. Nobody else is free, so I take him round the club.

3.00 pm I go home for a couple of hours' rest because I'm back at the club this evening to make sure a celebrity night I've organized goes well.

9.00 pm I'm back at the club now and it's packed – everyone seems to be having a great time!

Recording Engineer

What is a recording engineer?

Recording engineers are **technicians** who produce sound and video for CDs, vinyl and DVDs. Technical advances in the music industry mean that today many top music releases are not simply sound recordings but also DVDs and videos. This means that people not only can hear their favourite performers, but can see them in action as well.

Recording falls into two areas – sound and video. Most of the sound tracks are made in recording studios containing the most advanced electronic and digital sound recording, editing and playback equipment.

A recording engineer works at a mixing desk in a sound recording studio. The desk is used in multitrack recording in which the final soundtrack is made by the overlaying of a number of separate tracks.

Video engineers work both on location and in the studio. Here Jennifer Lopez films a music video in New York City in 2002.

Sound engineers are in charge of recording studios. Their technical ability and knowledge of music guarantees that the final sound is of the highest quality and takes advantage of the latest techniques. Recording studios usually specialize in recording a particular type of music such as popular music, classical music or film music.

Video engineers film music videos in a variety of locations. A great deal of thought and planning goes into the creation of these videos. They usually contain exciting and unusual visual effects to try to attract attention and stand out as different from other videos on the market.

Main tasks of a recording engineer

The job of a recording engineer has a very glamorous image and there are more people wanting work than there are jobs for them. Even very large recording studios employ only a few technical staff. Most recording engineers are associated with particular studios but, when more engineers are needed for a particular job, freelance workers are brought in.

Sound engineers are often also recording producers. This means they have considerable control over the finished product.

Recording engineers work closely with singers and songwriters who come up with the original ideas for recordings. The engineers' job is to give them advice on what is and what is not possible from a technical point of view.

Good points and bad points

'At school I was interested in science. I was also keen on music and played with a band for several years. I decided to combine the two and train as a sound engineer.

'Sometimes I worry about doing something wrong during a recording, such as forgetting to press a button, or failing to make the right adjustment to a piece of equipment, but so far I've been lucky.'

Sound engineers:

- set up the equipment in the studios and prepare them for the recording, deciding where the musicians will stand and positioning the **microphones**;
- operate the equipment used to record, **synchronize** and mix recordings;
- carry out **post-production** work, which is needed to achieve the final sound – usually a combination of different recordings and sound effects.

Engineers combine tapes, cut out unwanted sections and make sure the finished recording is the right length.

By mixing and manipulating different musical sounds, an engineer can have a huge impact on the final recording.

Video engineers:

- operate video cameras and other equipment, such as monitors and screens;
- check the lighting before filming begins and ensure that everything on the set is in place and ready;
- edit the video when filming is complete, removing and adding sections where necessary. The use of computerized equipment means a great deal of work is done at the post-production stage, after shooting has been completed.

Skills needed to be a recording engineer

Advanced technical and computer skills
Engineers need to be well-qualified and familiar with a wide range of different recording and editing equipment, such as multitrack recorders and digital editing systems. They have to know how to use the equipment safely and confidently.

A good ear and knowledge of music
Sound engineers in particular need to understand the types of sounds that are required and be able to judge the quality of the recording.

Quick thinking
Recording is an expensive business and any delays that occur will add to the costs. If difficulties do arise, engineers must deal with them quickly and efficiently.

Teamwork
Engineers work with creative people such as musicians, composers and directors as well as with other technical staff. It is important that they all work successfully together.

Patience
Although the finished recording may only last for a few minutes, hours of work go into making it. Engineers must be prepared to do a great deal of detailed work over a long period of time.

Equipment has to be monitored to make sure it is working properly. This engineer is working on classical music tracks for the acclaimed German recording label, Deutsche Grammophon Gesellschaft.

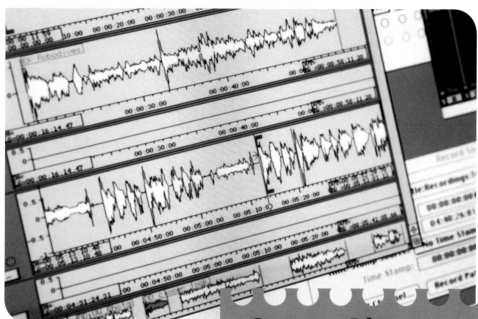

In the past, sound engineers would have literally to cut and splice recording tape to edit music tracks. Now engineers can edit soundtracks digitally on computer.

fact file

Most recording engineers have a degree in a subject such as broadcasting or sound engineering. Even with good qualifications, the way in is at the bottom, often as a runner, which means doing any odd jobs that come along.

Commitment

The work is not very secure and engineers need to take whatever jobs come along. This can mean a lot of travelling and working long, irregular hours. It is important for engineers to build up a reputation for being skilled and reliable because that is the way they will be offered further work.

Communication skills

Engineers often have to explain technical information to people who do not have their level of knowledge.

A day in the life of a recording engineer

Ben Wickham

Ben is a sound engineer with a small recording company. On leaving school he took a course in technical operations at college. This was a practical course during which he learned to operate the equipment used in radio, television and recording studios.

8.30 am It's an early start, because we have a full day's recording ahead. There's a lot of work to be done checking the equipment before we start.

9.30 am The music crew begin to arrive and want to limber up. The studio isn't huge and it's starting to feel crowded.

10.15 am A recording schedule has been drawn up. We'll be making a number of different recordings and putting them together afterwards. This way we can achieve some unusual sound effects. It also saves us money because it makes a few singers sound like a large group, so that's good from a financial point of view.

11.15 am I run a final check on the equipment then recording starts. I spend my time making sure my recording equipment is working properly.

2.30 pm I'm still at work. It's hot and not easy to concentrate. There's pressure on everyone to get the recording finished because recording studios are booked by the day. To run over would mean a lot of extra expense. This may not matter to top stars, but with artists who are struggling to make a name for themselves, budgets are limited.

4.00 pm   The musicians leave us to it. We're moving into the highly technical stuff, playing back recordings, synchronizing and mixing them.

4.30 pm   I'm beginning to feel hungry – I haven't eaten all day.

6.00 pm   One of the runners nips out for some take-away food. We're still working on the post-production stage. I really enjoy this because it's very satisfying to make a completely new sound.

8.00 pm   The runner returns with our food. We call it a day, and will carry on tomorrow.

In a recording studio, a singer wears headphones so that she can hear what the final recording will sound like, and so that she can communicate with the recording engineer.

The finished product reaches the shops. Teenagers buy CDs at a music store in Austin, Texas.

weblinks

For more information on a career as a recording engineer, go to www.waylinks.co.uk/series/soyouwant/musicanddance

Glossary

amplification – increasing a sound or making it louder, usually with the use of electrical equipment.

amplifier – an electronic device used to increase the strength of the signal fed into it and thereby make it louder.

audition – a test at which a performer or musician is asked to show his or her ability for a particular role or part.

bridge – the piece of wood that supports the strings on the main body of a stringed instrument such as a guitar or violin.

chamber group – a small orchestra of about 25 players, used normally for classical music work.

clog dancing – a dance in which the performer wears heavy wooden, or wooden-soled, shoes.

conductor – a person who conducts an orchestra or choir. Conductors use the movements of their hands or, more usually, a baton (thin stick) to guide the players.

contract – a business document that states the terms of agreement between two or more people.

corps de ballet – the group of dancers who perform together supporting the soloists who dance alone.

hip-hop – a popular type of music where rhymes are recited to music. It has its roots in reggae music.

improvise – to make something up as you go along.

microphone – an instrument which is able to pick up sounds and make them louder.

mixes – combinations of different types of music mixed together electronically by a DJ.

mixing desk – the most important piece of equipment for a DJ, used for balancing and adjusting sound levels and combining sounds.

musical theory – the rules and principles of music. The study of how music is created and performed.

notation – system used for writing music down.

pegs – the pins at the head of an instrument, for example a violin, cello or guitar, which are used to lengthen and shorten the strings.

peripatetic – moving around. Peripatetic music teachers travel to several different schools to teach pupils.

pitch – the sound of notes of music in relation to other notes, for example, high pitch (high notes) or low pitch (low notes).

pliable – easily moulded or bent.

post-production – work carried out on a piece of music after it has been produced. This might include adding backing sounds or special effects.

reggae – a type of African Caribbean music developed in Jamaica. Its popularity spread with the music of reggae artists such as Bob Marley.

score – the written or printed form of a piece of music, showing the different instrumental or vocal parts.

soldering – joining pieces of metal together by melting an alloy (a metal mixture) so that it forms a thin layer between them.

step dancing – a dance in which a display of different steps is more important than gesture or posture.

synchronize – to bring two things together and cause them to happen at exactly the same time.

technician – someone skilled in doing a practical type of job.

tenacious – tough, stubborn or persistent.

welding – attaching pieces of metal together by softening them with heat and hammering.

Further Information

So do you still want to work in music or dance?

This book aims to give you an idea of the range of different jobs in these areas, and what working in them is really like. After having read this book you can perhaps see the difference between enjoying music or dance as a hobby and setting out to become a professional performer.

It takes a great deal of talent, hard work, energy, determination and luck to succeed in taking up music or dance professionally. If you feel that a normal routine and the security of a regular salary are going to be important to you, possibly you are one of those people for whom music or dance is going to be a rewarding hobby rather than a career.

There are many other careers in music and dance that have not been covered in detail in this book, such as working as a choreographer, creating dance routines, or as a composer, writing music. These careers, like the others covered in the book, are difficult to enter.

The chances are that if you are considering a career as a performance artist, such as a musician or a dancer, you will already be taking lessons. The best person to advise you on a future career is likely to be your music or dance teacher.

If you are at secondary school and seriously interested in a career as a music teacher, promotions manager, instrument maker or recording engineer, ask your careers teacher if he or she could arrange for some work experience. This means spending some time, usually a week or two, with a person doing the work, so you can see for yourself exactly what it is like.

Books

If you want to find out about working in music or dance, you will find the following helpful:

How to Succeed in the Music Business, written by Allan Dann and John Underwood, published by Virgin Books, 2002.

Careers in Music, written by Mark Edgley Smith and Ruth Yockney, published by Kogan Page, 1999.

Working in Music, published by Connexions, 2004.

Working in the Performing Arts, published by Connexions, 2003.

weblinks▸

For websites relevant to this book, go to www.waylinks.co.uk/ series/soyouwant/ musicanddance

Useful addresses

Dance

United Kingdom

British Ballet Organization
Woolborough House
39 Lonsdale Road
Barnes
London SW13 9JP
Tel: 020 8748 1241

British Theatre Dance
Association
The International Arts
Centre
Garden Street
Leicester LE1 3UA
Tel: 0116 262 2279

Royal Academy of Dance
36 Battersea Square
London SW11 3RA

Scottish Ballet
261 West Princes Street
Glasgow
Tel: 0141 331 2931

Australia

Royal Academy of Dance
Australia
www.rad.org.au

New Zealand

Royal Academy of Dance
New Zealand
Level 5 Xacta Tower
94 Dixon Street (PO Box
11-718)
Wellington

South Africa

Dance Societies and
Dance Associations in
South Africa
www.dancedirectory.co.za

Music

United Kingdom

Incorporated Society of
Musicians
10 Stratford Place
London W1C 1AA
Tel: 020 7629 4413

Royal Academy of Music
Marylebone Road
London NW1 5HT
Tel: 020 7873 7373

Royal Scottish Academy of
Music and Drama
100 Renfrew Street
Glasgow G2 3DB
Tel: 0141 332 4101

Instrument Making and Repair

Institute of Musical
Instrument Technology
Northfield House
11 Kendal Avenue South
Sanderstead
CR2 0QR

Recording Engineering

Skillset
Prospect House
80-110 New Oxford Street
London WC1A 1HB
Tel: 020 7520 5757

Teaching Music

Teacher Training Agency
Portland House
Stag Place
London SW1E 5TT
Tel: 01245 454454

Australia

Australia National
Academy of Music
www.anam.unimelb.edu.au

National Training
Information Service
Australian National
Training Authority
Level 17, 200 Mary Street
Brisbane QLD 4001
GPO Box 3120
Tel: (07) 3246 2300

National Training
Information Service
5/321 Exhibition Street
Melbourne VIC 3000
GPO Box 5347BB
Melbourne VIC 3001
Tel: (03) 9630 9800

New Zealand

Associated Board of the
Royal Schools of Music of
New Zealand
www.abrsm.org.nz

kiwicareers.govt.nz
Tel: 0800 222733

Index